For information contact: Enna, Inc., www.enna.com

The VSM Participant Workbook and Design are trademarks of Enna, In

T0265179

International Standard Book Number: 9781138069565

Distributed by Productivity Press, an imprint of CRC Press
711 Third Avenue, New York, NY 10017
2 Park Square, Milton Park, Abingdon, Oxon OX14 4RN
www.productivitypress.com

CRC Press is an imprint of the Taylor & Francis Group, an informa business

---

Note:
This publication contains the opinions and ideas of its authors. It is intended to provide helpful and informative material on the subject matter provided. It is sold with the understanding that the authors and publisher are not engaged in rendering professional services in this book. If the reader requires personal assistance or counsel, a competent professional should be consulted.

The authors and publisher specifically disclaim any responsibility for any liability, loss, or risk, personal or otherwise, which is incurred as a consequence, directly or indirectly, of the use and application of any of the contents of this book.

Special Symbols:

This workbook is organized to help guide the individual through the training. In addition to the Notes section there are a number of symbols used to help the participant throughout the presentation and workshop. For your convenience these symbols are repeated at the introduction of each section of this workbook.

Suggestion:

This symbol represents a general suggestion relating to your involvement in the presentation and workshop.

Tip:

This symbol represents a tip to the participant which is specific to the subject being taught.

Question:

This symbol represents a question that may be directed to the participant, or meant for the participant to reflect on during the presentation and workshop.

Table of Contents:

.

Participant Workbook

Introduction

- Introduction to the Workshop
- The History of Value Stream Mapping - VSM
- The Purpose of Value Stream Mapping
- High Level Benefits of Value Stream Mapping

Participant Workbook Provided To:

_____

 Suggestion **Tip** **Question**

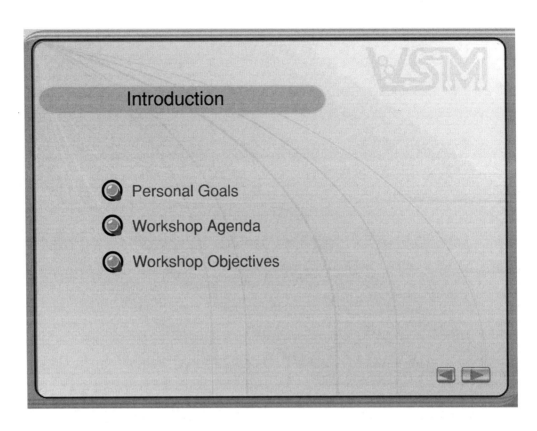

Notes, Slide 2:

_____

_____

_____

_____

_____

Suggestion:
Write your personal
goal for the workshop
in the Notes section.

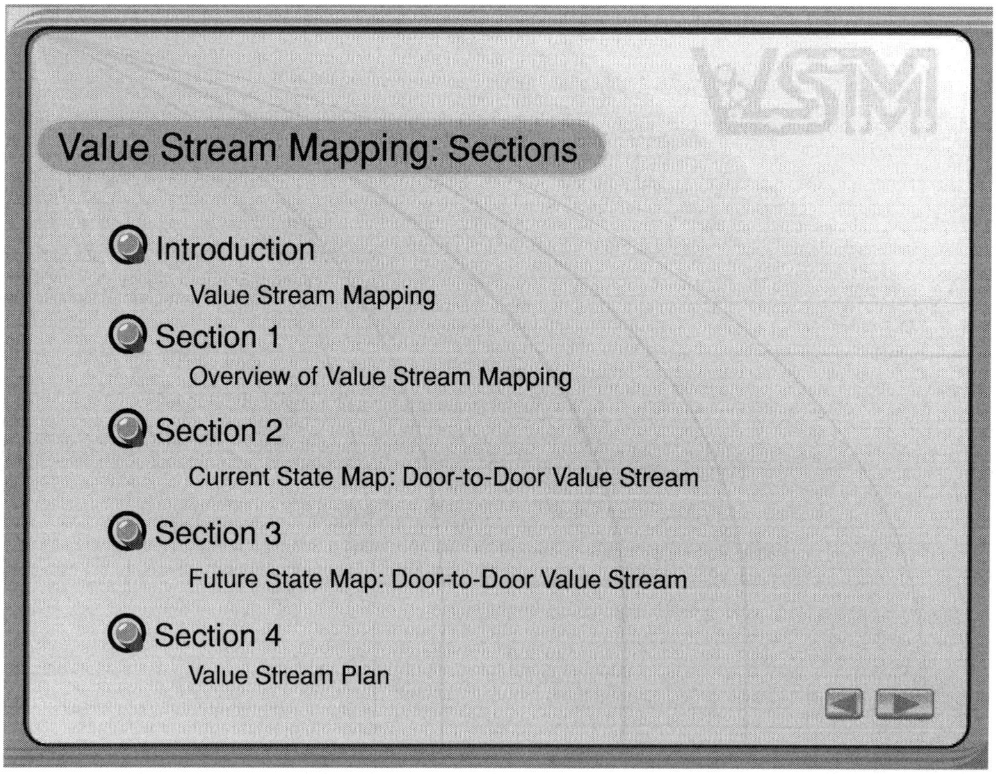

Notes, Slide 3:

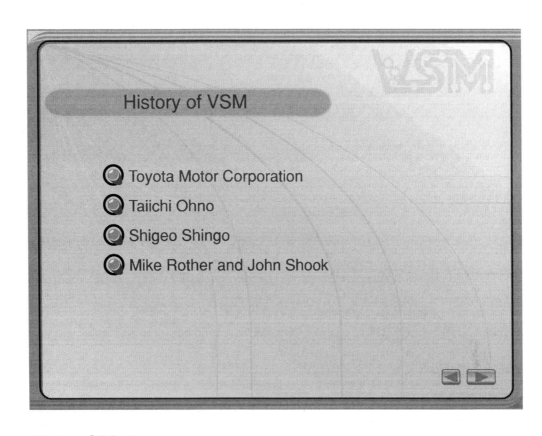

Notes, Slide 4:

_____

_____

_____

_____

_____

_____

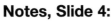

Tip:
Value stream mapping establishes an implementation plan based on Lean principles.

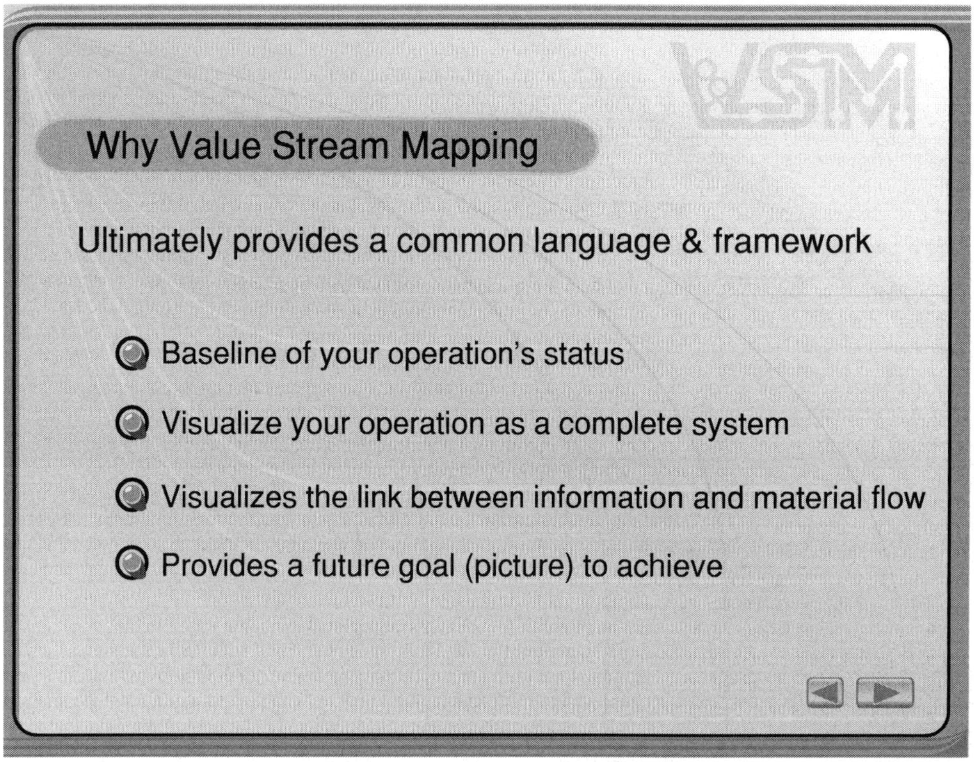

Why Value Stream Mapping

Ultimately provides a common language & framework

- Baseline of your operation's status
- Visualize your operation as a complete system
- Visualizes the link between information and material flow
- Provides a future goal (picture) to achieve

Notes, Slide 5:

_____

_____

_____

_____

_____

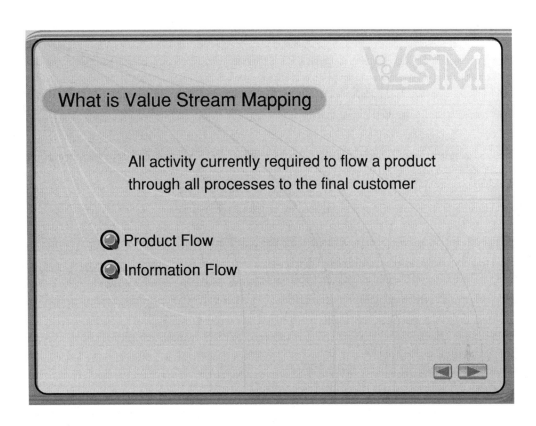

What is Value Stream Mapping

All activity currently required to flow a product
through all processes to the final customer

- Product Flow
- Information Flow

Notes, Slide 6:

_____

_____

_____

_____

_____

_____

Tip:
_At this point we are
only discussing the
high-level purpose of
value stream map-
ping. We will become
concerned with the
details later in the
workshop._

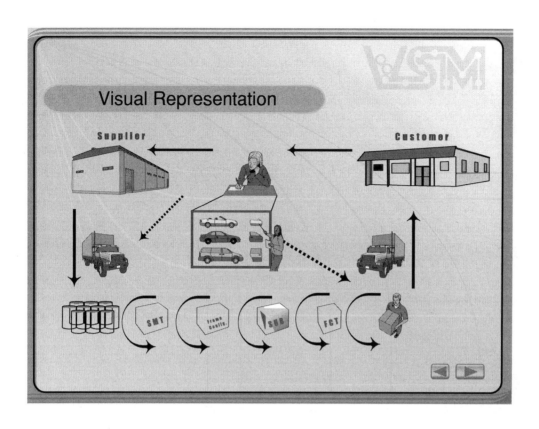

Notes, Slide 7:

_____

_____

_____

_____

_____

_____

Question:
What is the goal of developing a Current State Map?

_____

_____

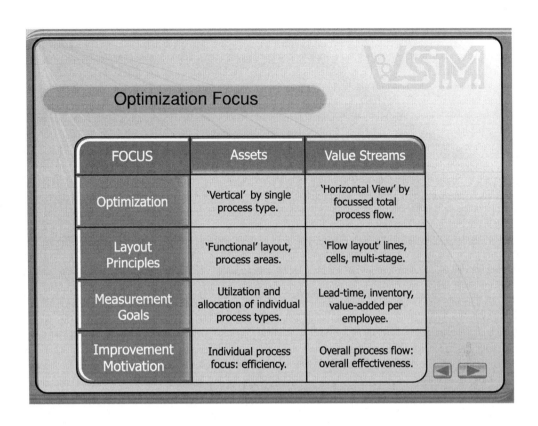

Notes, Slide 8:

_____

_____

_____

_____

_____

_____

Question:
What are some benefits of looking at the entire operational system?

_____

_____

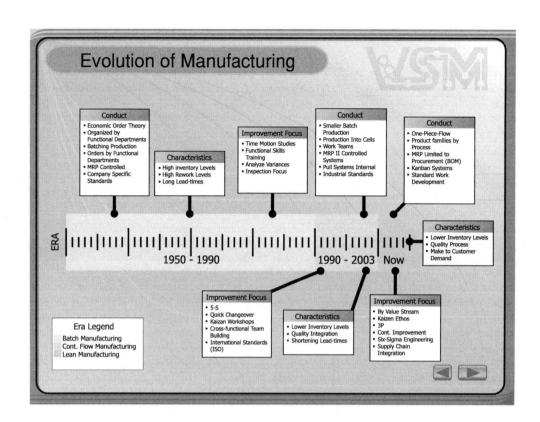

Notes, Slide 9:

_____

_____

_____

_____

_____

_____

Tip:
Lean manufacturing is relatively new, however it is necessary to adopt Lean manufacturing the methods are more effective then past ones.

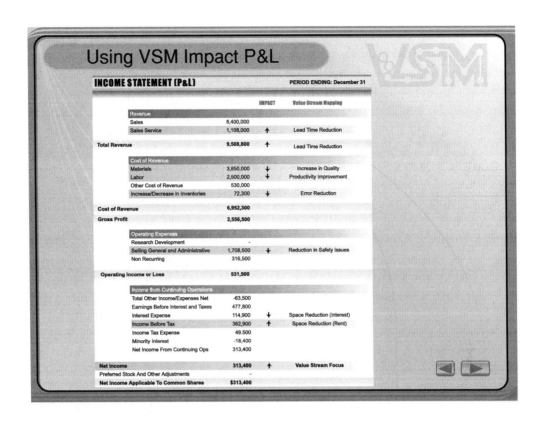

Notes, Slide 10:

_____

_____

_____

_____

_____

_____

Suggestion:
Offer your input throughout the presentation. Each participant is encouraged to contribute to the workshop.

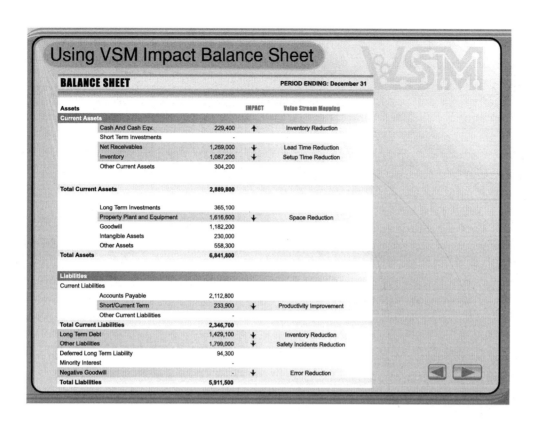

Using VSM Impact Balance Sheet

BALANCE SHEET			PERIOD ENDING: December 31	
Assets		**IMPACT**	**Value Stream Mapping**	
Current Assets				
Cash And Cash Eqv.	229,400	↑	Inventory Reduction	
Short Term Investments	-			
Net Receivables	1,269,000	↓	Lead Time Reduction	
Inventory	1,087,200	↓	Setup Time Reduction	
Other Current Assets	304,200			
Total Current Assets	**2,889,800**			
Long Term Investments	365,100			
Property Plant and Equipment	1,616,600	↓	Space Reduction	
Goodwill	1,182,200			
Intangible Assets	230,000			
Other Assets	558,300			
Total Assets	**6,841,800**			
Liabilities				
Current Liabilities				
Accounts Payable	2,112,800			
Short/Current Term	233,900	↓	Productivity Improvement	
Other Current Liabilities	-			
Total Current Liabilities	**2,346,700**			
Long Term Debt	1,429,100	↓	Inventory Reduction	
Other Liabilities	1,799,000	↓	Safety Incidents Reduction	
Deferred Long Term Liability	94,300			
Minority Interest				
Negative Goodwill	-	↓	Error Reduction	
Total Liabilities	**5,911,500**			

Notes, Slide 11:

_____

_____

_____

_____

_____

_____

Benefits of Value Stream Mapping

- Through Direct Observation
  - Overall work flow
  - Link between information and material flow
  - High impact areas for improvement
  - The 7 Wastes of Operations

Notes, Slide 12:

_____

_____

_____

_____

_____

_____

Tip:
This workshop is structured as a teach-do format. This means that you will learn concepts and then apply them as you analyze your value streams.

Tip:
Take time to ask your Facilitator for examples and write them down. You will need to recognize these wastes as you analyze your value streams.

Notes, Slide 13:

<u>Waiting:</u> When material, information, machines or approvals are not ready.

<u>Motion:</u> Any movement related to people that does not add value to the product or service.

<u>Transportation:</u> Moving material from one area of the company to the other.

<u>Inventory:</u> Any material in the area other than what is immediately needed for the next process/stage/step.

<u>Overproduction:</u> Making more products or components than the next internal or external customer needs.

<u>Processing:</u> Activity that adds no value to the product or service from the viewpoint of the internal/external customer.

<u>Defects:</u> Making bad parts, having scrap material, the wrong information and/or having to rework items.

Tip:
Remember these definitions as they are the most accurate versions translated from the Japanese originals.

_____

_____

_____

_____

_____

_____

Section 1
Overview

Participant Workbook

Section 1

- The Scope of Value Stream Mapping
- Key Value Stream Definitions
- Illustrated Examples of the Current and Future State Maps
- Summarizing the Value Stream Perspective

 Suggestion   **Tip**   **Question**

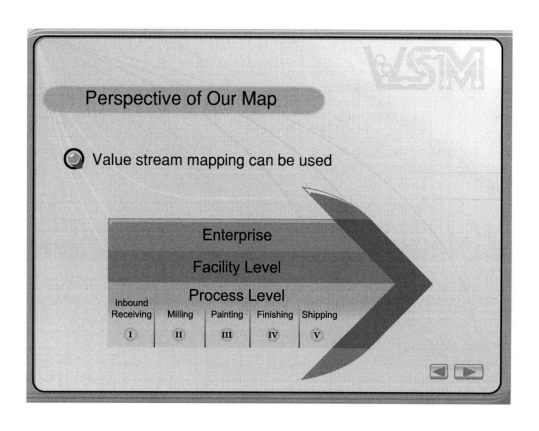

Notes, Slide 15:

_____

_____

_____

_____

_____

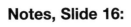

Value Stream Mapping Defined

- Value Stream: all the activities, value-added and others, needed to make a completed product
  - Value Stream Map: a set of drawings that make the flow of material and information visible
    - Value Stream Mapping: describes the activities that create these drawings
      - Current State Map: illustrates the process as it is today
        - Future State Map: illustrates the ideal state by applying Lean manufacturing methodology

Notes, Slide 16:

_____

_____

_____

_____

_____

_____

Tip:
Take time to fully understand these definitions. They are the basis for understanding value stream mapping.

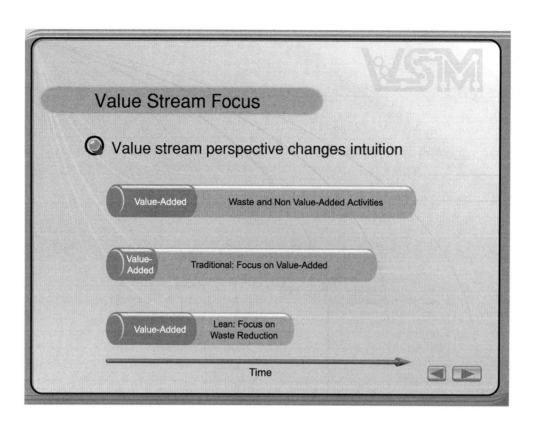

Notes, Slide 17:

_____

_____

_____

_____

_____

_____

Suggestion:
Provide feedback when asked by the Facilitator. This inter-action encourages group learning.

Question:
Please provide two examples of value added and non-value added activities in your department.

_____

_____

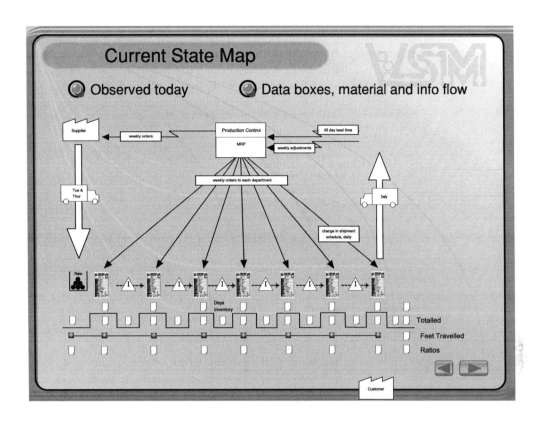

Notes, Slide 18:

_____

_____

_____

_____

_____

_____

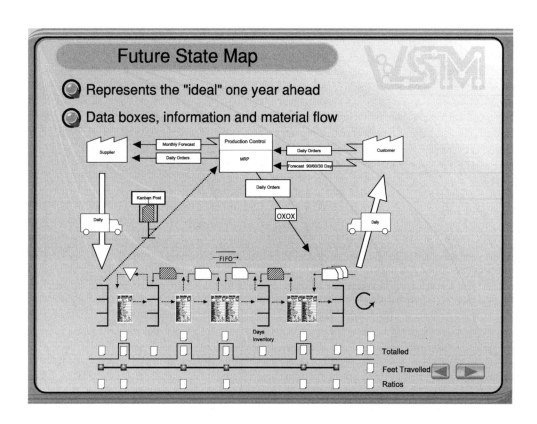

Notes, Slide 19:

_____

_____

_____

_____

_____

Tip:
The power of value stream mapping is in the use of the tools that create each map. Using the tools results in an overall picture that all members can focus on and identify improvements.

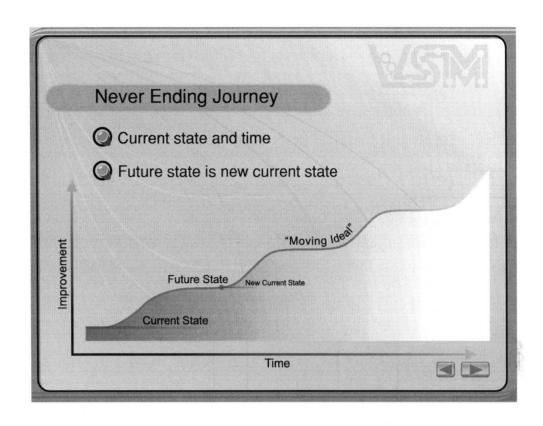

Notes, Slide 20:

_____

_____

_____

_____

_____

_____

Tip:
Value stream mapping is a continuous tool used by a company to improve.

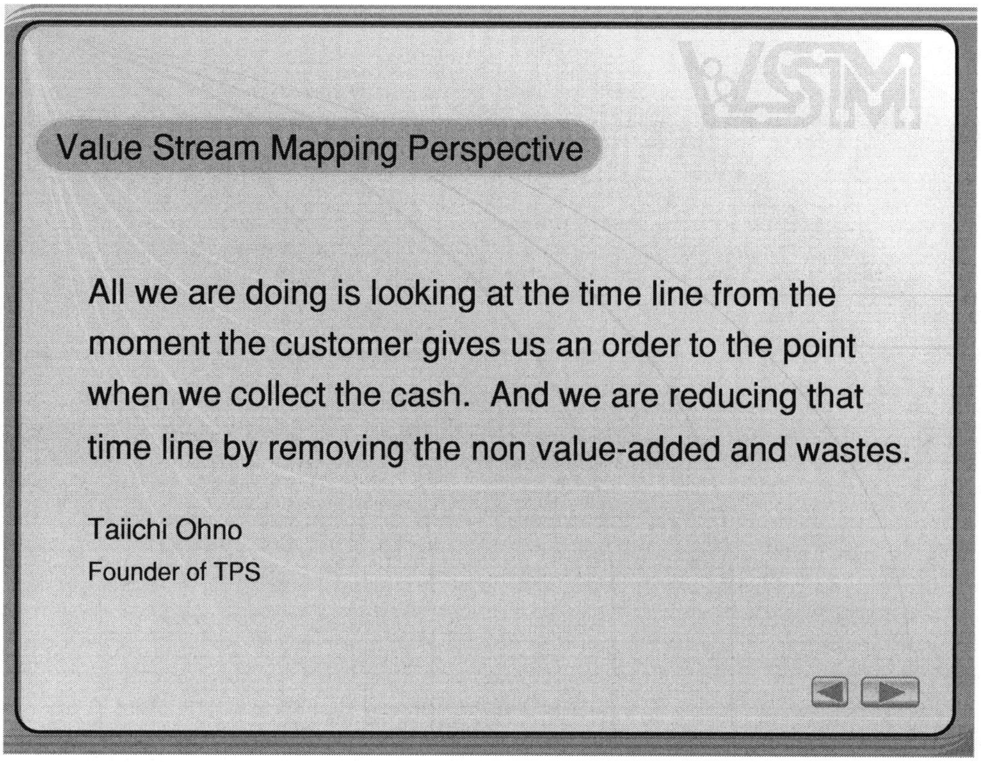

Value Stream Mapping Perspective

All we are doing is looking at the time line from the moment the customer gives us an order to the point when we collect the cash. And we are reducing that time line by removing the non value-added and wastes.

Taiichi Ohno
Founder of TPS

Notes, Slide 21:

_____

_____

_____

_____

_____

_____

Question:
As you read this quote, what value do you see in the statement?

_____

_____

Section 2

Current State Map
Door-to-Door Value Stream

Participant Workbook

Section 2

- The Nine Steps to Value Stream Mapping
- The Analytical Tools and Gathering Information
- VSM Data Boxes
- Observing, Collecting, and Creating the Current State Map

 Suggestion **Tip** **Question**

Current State Activities

1. Identify Primary Value Streams
2. Identify Key Metrics
3. Map Overall Process Flow
4. Complete Data Boxes
5. Draw Inventory and Day Supply
6. Summarize Timelines
7. Calculate Ratios
8. Illustrate Information Flow
9. Kaizen Bursts

Notes, Slide 23:

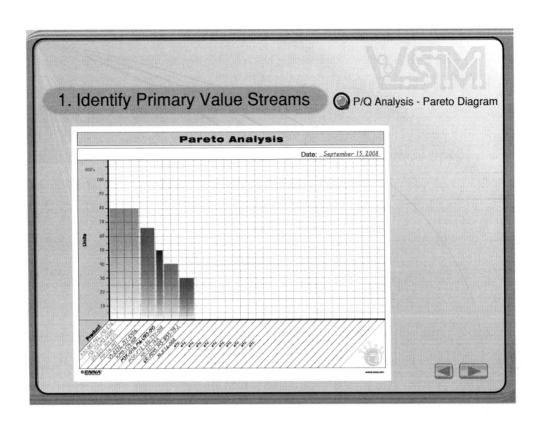

Notes, Slide 24:

_____

_____

_____

_____

_____

_____

Tip:
The Pareto Analysis
illustrates quantity
and type of products.

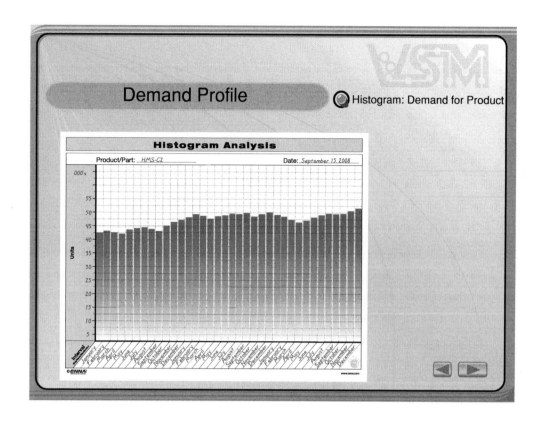

Suggestion:
When making charts use brightly colored markers. The charts made in the work-shop may be used in future presentations.

Notes, Slide 25:

Tip:
The Histogram Analysis form consid-ers cyclical changes in product demand.

Notes, Slide 26:

_____

_____

_____

_____

_____

_____

Tip:
The Product Family Matrix form is used to group products by similar processes.

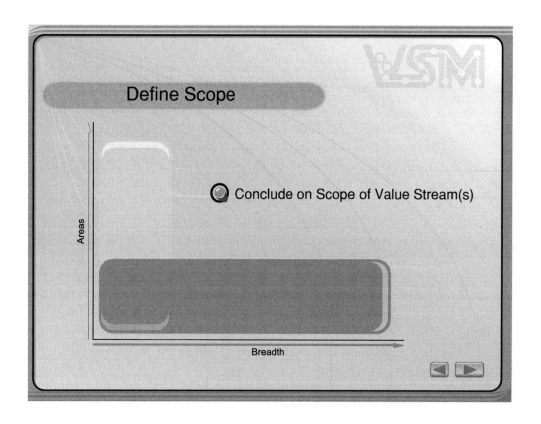

Notes, Slide 27:

_____

_____

_____

_____

_____

_____

Tip:
Provide your input as the team decides on the scope of work for this workshop.

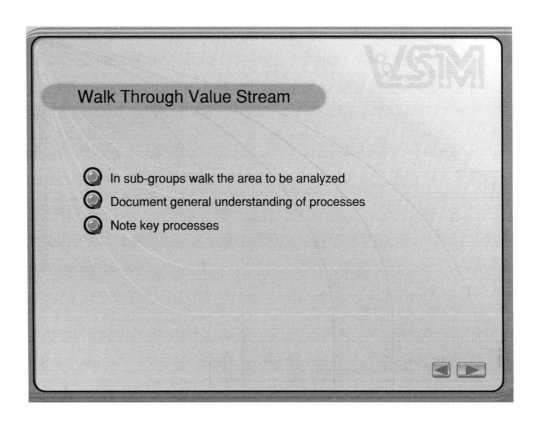

Walk Through Value Stream

- In sub-groups walk the area to be analyzed
- Document general understanding of processes
- Note key processes

Notes, Slide 28:

_____

_____

_____

_____

_____

_____

Tip:
Work in small groups of two or three as you walk the value streams.

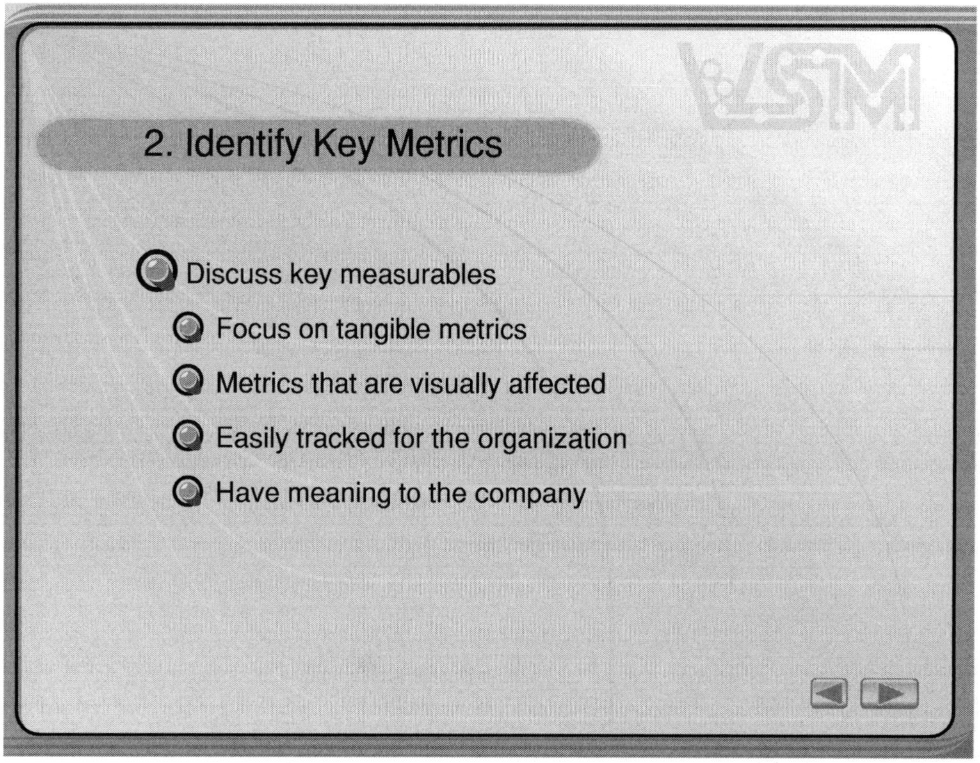

2. Identify Key Metrics

- Discuss key measurables
  - Focus on tangible metrics
  - Metrics that are visually affected
  - Easily tracked for the organization
  - Have meaning to the company

Notes, Slide 29:

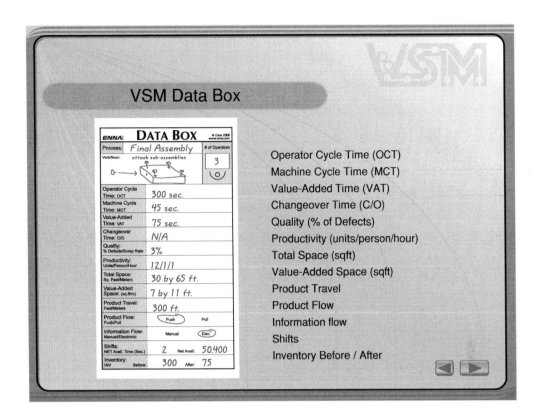

Notes, Slide 30:

Operator Cycle Time: The actual hands-on time the operator is involved in the process, from when a part is picked up to when it is set down.

Machine Cycle Time: The machine processing time; however, this does not include the changeover of a machine, just the cycle time. If there are multiple parts note the time and lot size. It is important to note whether OCT and MCT are summed during the observation, or if the OCT takes place as the machine is operating. If it does, than the longer of the two times needs to be noted. As well, if the OCT and MCT are performed in series then the total of both need to be added together; this would then be the true total process time.

Value-Added Time: The portion of time when the part or product is actually changing form; it is the portion of time that the customer is actually paying for.

Tip:
Take time to review the Commandments for Improvement poster.

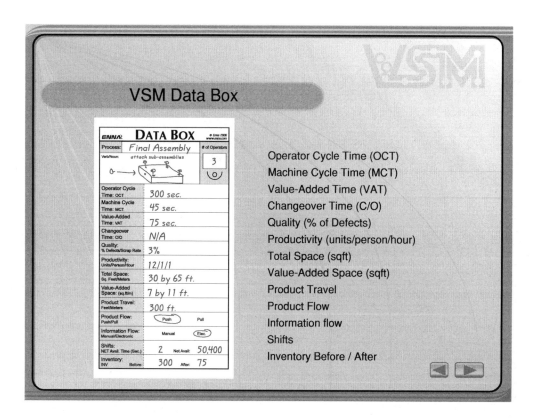

Operator Cycle Time (OCT)
Machine Cycle Time (MCT)
Value-Added Time (VAT)
Changeover Time (C/O)
Quality (% of Defects)
Productivity (units/person/hour)
Total Space (sqft)
Value-Added Space (sqft)
Product Travel
Product Flow
Information flow
Shifts
Inventory Before / After

Notes, Slide 30, Continued:

<u>Changeover Time:</u> The time it takes to changeover the machine from the last good part of the previous production run to the first good part from the new run. Note this time and ask for information on changeover time if you are not able to observe it.

<u>Quality:</u> The percentage of non-conforming parts per lot or production run. This includes the scrap at the beginning and end of the production run. Make sure to ask the operators what kind of scrap and defects they get per run.

<u>Productivity:</u> Measured as units or products per person per hour. This is a labor productivity measurement. You may be able to get hands-on measurements or look at past data to get an understanding of this measurement.

Tip:
The Data Box is the building block for your current state map. Use as many of the measurements as you can.

VSM Data Box

ENNA	**DATA BOX**	© Enna 2006 www.enna.com
Process:	*Final Assembly*	# of Operators
Verb/Noun:	*attach sub-assemblies*	**3**

Operator Cycle Time: OCT	*300 sec.*
Machine Cycle Time: MCT	*45 sec.*
Value-Added Time: VAT	*75 sec.*
Changeover Time: C/O	*N/A*
Quality: % Defects/Scrap Rate	*3%*
Productivity: Units/Person/Hour	*12/1/1*
Total Space: Sq. Feet/Meters	*30 by 65 ft.*
Value-Added Space: (sq.ft/m)	*7 by 11 ft.*
Product Travel: Feet/Meters	*300 ft.*
Product Flow: Push/Pull	Push / Pull
Information Flow: Manual/Electronic	Manual / Elec.
Shifts: NET Avail. Time (Sec.)	*2* Net Avail: *50,400*
Inventory: INV Before:	*300* After: *75*

Operator Cycle Time (OCT)
Machine Cycle Time (MCT)
Value-Added Time (VAT)
Changeover Time (C/O)
Quality (% of Defects)
Productivity (units/person/hour)
Total Space (sqft)
Value-Added Space (sqft)
Product Travel
Product Flow
Information flow
Shifts
Inventory Before / After

Notes, Slide 30, Continued:

<u>Total Space:</u> The total foot print of an area used to produce a part. This includes storage, machine and work areas. It is a square foot measurement, so please measure the length and width of the area.

<u>Value-Added Space:</u> The actual space where value-added activity occurs; usually this is about six inches greater than the actual product. Remember, just because a machine is large does not mean it is value-added space.

<u>Product Travel:</u> The total linear feet travelled by the product. This includes placing the product or part into the machine or placing the product back into a box or onto a shelf. Trace the total distance travelled to gain a useful measurement as to how many feet an item travels during the manufacturing processes.

<u>Product Flow:</u> The push or pull of a system; how orders are determined for production. Most of the time the current state is push.

Tip:
Note the definitions for each of the Data Box categories. When you are on the shop floor you will need to reference these definitions.

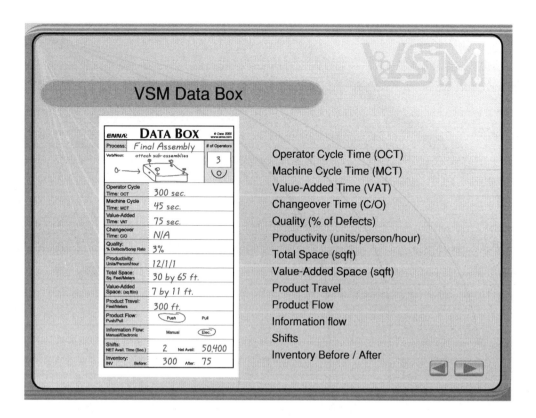

Notes, Slide 30, Continued:

<u>Information Flow:</u> Assesses whether the physical (hardcopy) or electronic information is pushed to the process step or if it is pulled.

<u>Shifts:</u> The quantity of shifts used in each process. This is essential when determining available time; available time is the time of a shift minus breaks and lunch/dinner. It is the time truly available to manufacture. This time is used to determine the Takt Time in the development of the future state.

<u>Inventory:</u> The current measurement of inventory in different areas. To establish a standard measure all the inventory in the area before and after the process. For inventory between processes, count the inventory before the process you are analyzing into your "before" inventory section. If all teams do this the inventory will not be double counted.

Tip:
Take time to make sure that no inventory is double counted.

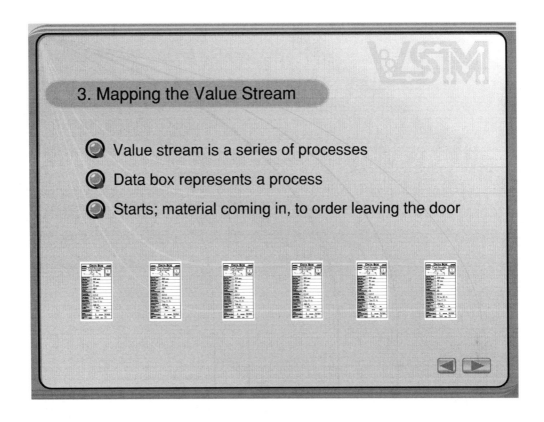

Notes, Slide 31:

_____

_____

_____

_____

_____

_____

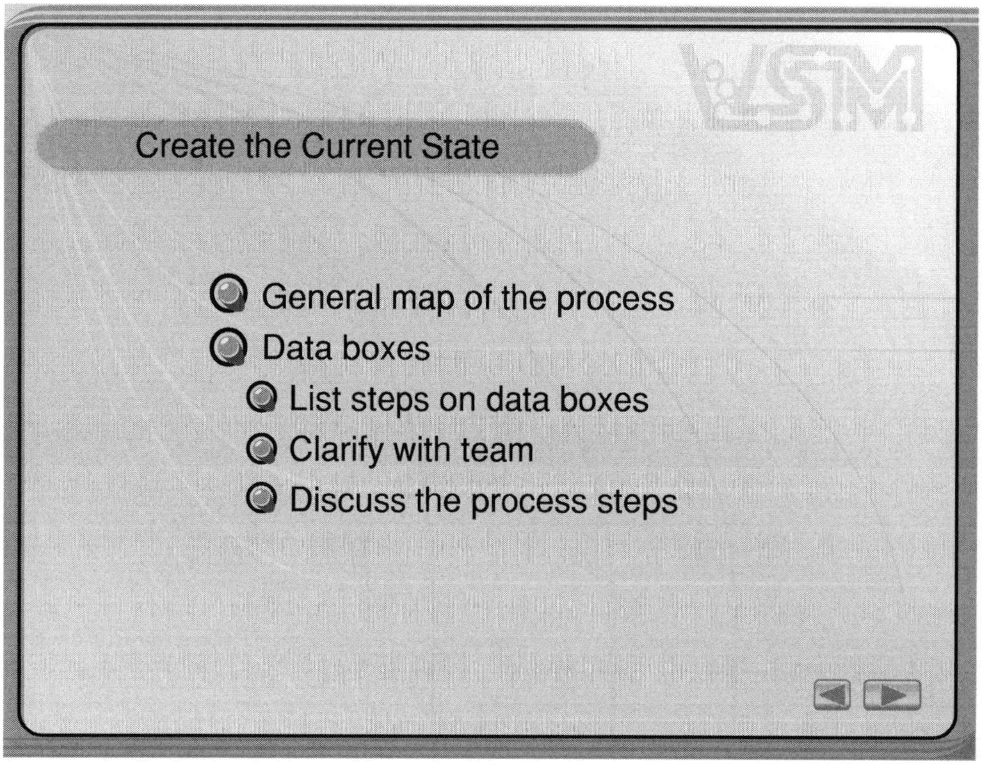

Create the Current State

- General map of the process
- Data boxes
  - List steps on data boxes
  - Clarify with team
  - Discuss the process steps

Notes, Slide 32:

Tip:
As you observe the the value stream take notes of the process and identify any processes that have not been discussed.

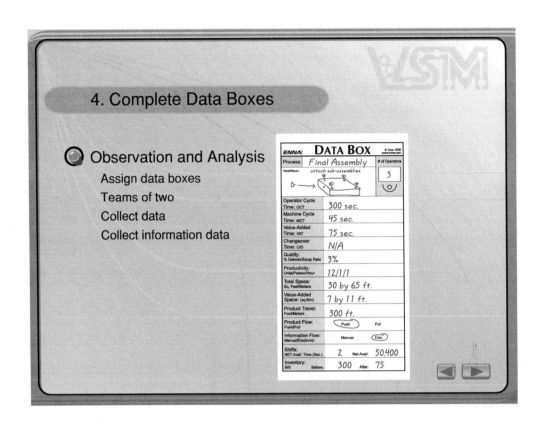

4. Complete Data Boxes

Observation and Analysis

- Assign data boxes
- Teams of two
- Collect data
- Collect information data

Notes, Slide 33:

_____

_____

_____

_____

_____

_____

Suggestion:
If you do not have enough activities assigned to you inform the Facilitator.

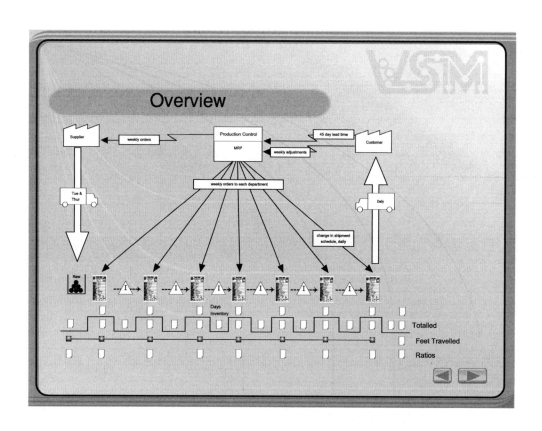

Notes, Slide 34:

_____

_____

_____

_____

_____

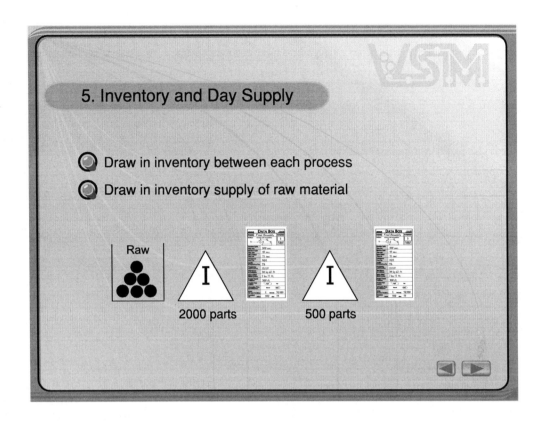

Notes, Slide 35:

_____

_____

_____

_____

_____

_____

Tip:
Use the value stream mapping symbols to link the processes together.

Question:
If there is a large batch of inventory in the process which Data Box field should it be counted in?

_____

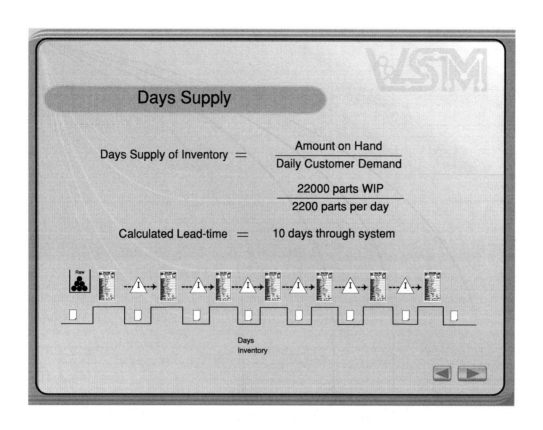

Notes, Slide 36:

_____

_____

_____

_____

_____

_____

Tip:
Double check your calculations for inventory days.

6. Summarize Timelines

- Summarize OCT & MCT = Cycle Times
- Summarize Value-Added Times

- Total Cycle Time
- Total Value-Added Times — Totals
- Total Inventory Days

Notes, Slide 37:

_____

_____

_____

_____

_____

_____

Tip:
Use post-it notes to summarize the times under each data box.

Question:
Value-added time is only the time that the product is actually changing to customers' specifications.

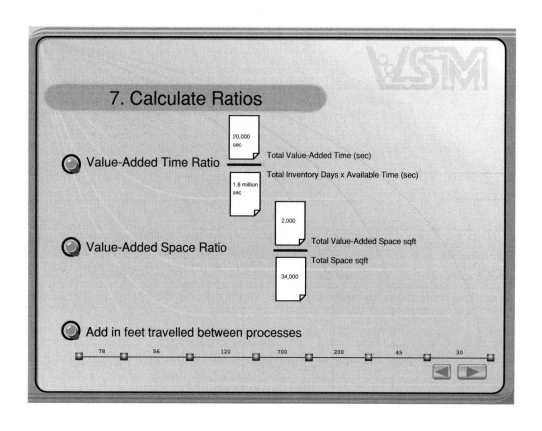

Notes, Slide 38:

_____

_____

_____

_____

_____

_____

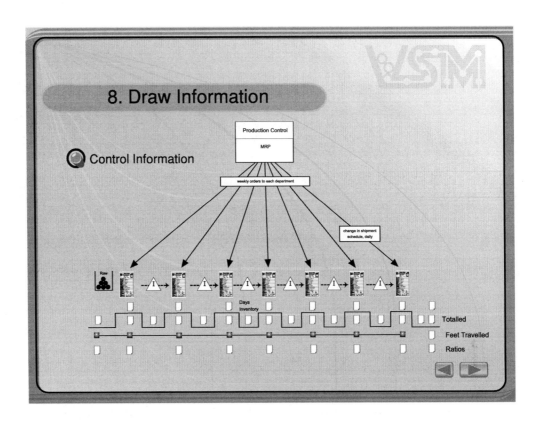

Notes, Slide 39:

_____

_____

_____

_____

_____

_____

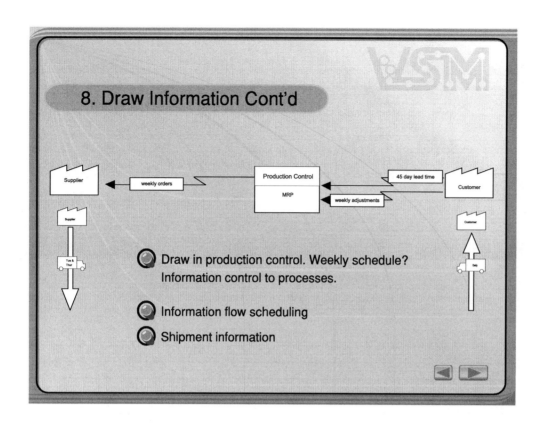

8. Draw Information Cont'd

Draw in production control. Weekly schedule?
Information control to processes.

Information flow scheduling

Shipment information

Notes, Slide 40:

_____

_____

_____

_____

_____

Tip:
When using the Kaizen Bursts only address issues that are within the value stream being discussed.

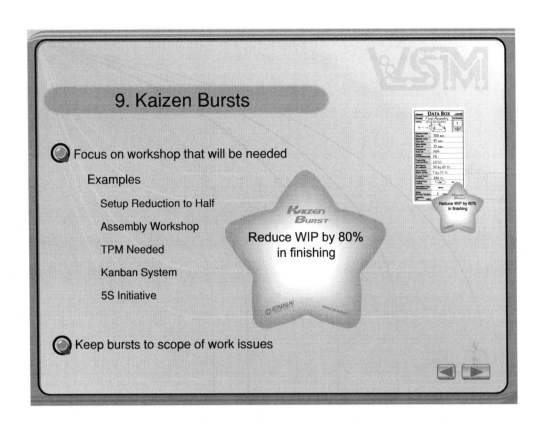

Notes, Slide 41:

_____

_____

_____

_____

_____

_____

Suggestion:
Verify that the information collected is the same as the information being summarized.

Section 3

Future State Map
Door-to-Door Value Stream

Participant Workbook

Section 3

- The Non-Value Perspective and Developing the Future State
- Takt Time and Future State Creation Explained
- The Kanban Systems and Supermarkets
- The Future State Map and One-Piece-Flow

 Suggestion **Tip** **Question**

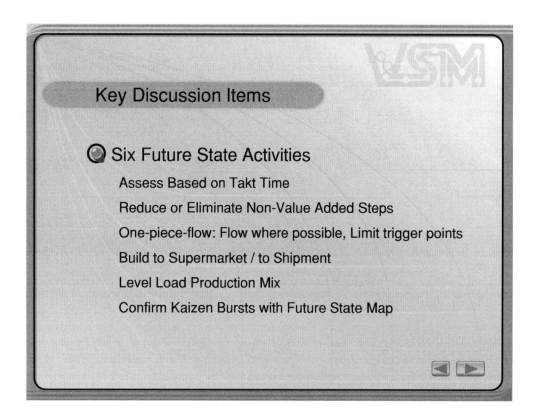

Key Discussion Items

Six Future State Activities

Assess Based on Takt Time

Reduce or Eliminate Non-Value Added Steps

One-piece-flow: Flow where possible, Limit trigger points

Build to Supermarket / to Shipment

Level Load Production Mix

Confirm Kaizen Bursts with Future State Map

Tip:
Following these six steps will create your future state map.

Notes, Slide 43:

_____

_____

_____

_____

_____

Tip:
Document the ideas that the group discusses with the kaizen bursts.

Calculate Takt Time

Synchronize operations

Takt time is the rate at which a product or component should be produced based on customer demand.

$$\text{Takt Time} = \frac{\text{Total available production time}}{\text{Total customer demand}}$$

This will effectively give you the rate of flow from one process to the next

Notes, Slide 44:

_____

_____

_____

_____

_____

_____

Suggestion:
This is a key slide. If you have any questions, please ask the Facilitator.

Question:
Why is Takt time so important when considering the design of a production system?

_____

_____

Calculate Takt Time

- This calculation provides insight into cell design and layout of the facility.
- We want to determine flow of product and scope of work for each operation.

$$\text{Takt Time} = \frac{27000}{216} = 125 \text{ sec/ finished part}$$

- Grinding needs to produce two parts per finished product so its Takt time is 62.5 sec/part. OCT is 35 sec including 5 sec load/unload. MCT is 40 seconds.
- We need to see if we can give the operator 27.5 sec more value-added work.

Notes, Slide 45:

_____

_____

_____

_____

_____

Calculate Takt Time

- This calculation provides insight into cell design and layout of the facility.
- We want to determine flow of product and scope of work for each operation.

$$\text{Takt Time} = \frac{27000}{216} = 125 \text{ sec/ finished part}$$

- Grinding needs to produce two parts per finished product so its Takt time is 62.5 sec/part. OCT is 35 sec including 5 sec load/unload. MCT is 40 seconds.
- We need to see if we can give the operator 27.5 sec more value-added work.

Notes, Slide 45, Continued:

Calculate Takt Time

- This calculation provides insight into cell design and layout of the facility.
- We want to determine flow of product and scope of work for each operation.

$$\text{Takt Time} = \frac{27000}{216} = 125 \text{ sec/ finished part}$$

- Grinding needs to produce two parts per finished product so its Takt time is 62.5 sec/part. OCT is 35 sec including 5 sec load/unload. MCT is 40 seconds.
- We need to see if we can give the operator 27.5 sec more value-added work.

Notes, Slide 45, Continued:

Question:
Balancing to Takt time reveals that some operations are too fast and this causes the operation to actually fall behind with what products are really needed.

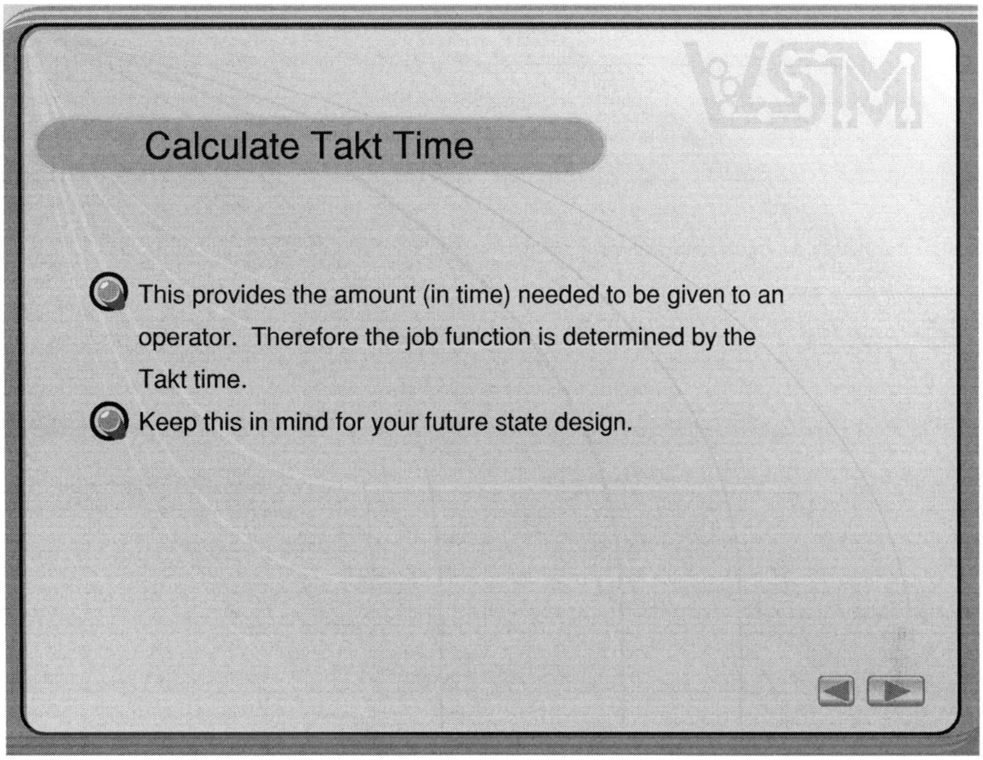

Calculate Takt Time

- This provides the amount (in time) needed to be given to an operator. Therefore the job function is determined by the Takt time.
- Keep this in mind for your future state design.

Notes, Slide 46:

_____

_____

_____

_____

_____

_____

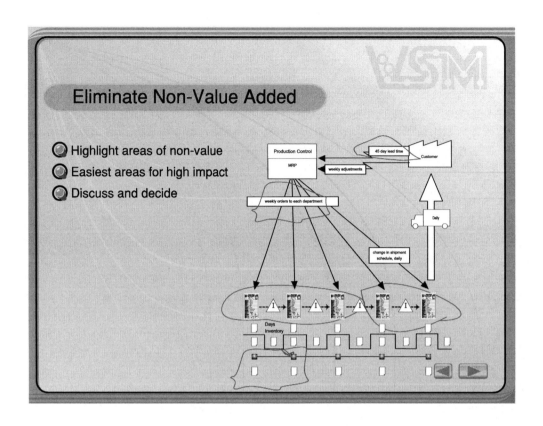

Eliminate Non-Value Added

- Highlight areas of non-value
- Easiest areas for high impact
- Discuss and decide

Notes, Slide 47:

_____

_____

_____

_____

_____

_____

Tip:
Use a red marker to highlight areas with the quickest and greatest improvement potential.

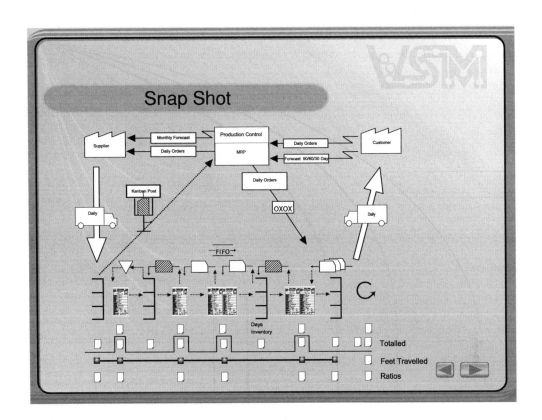

Notes, Slide 48:

_____

_____

_____

_____

_____

_____

Suggestion:
Discuss larger scope
issues with many
people as they may
have ideas that gen-
erate a better plan
and result.

Future State Map Creation

- Based on takt time and cycle time build new model
- Re-align data boxes bringing processes together

Notes, Slide 49:

_____

_____

_____

_____

_____

_____

Tip:
Discuss linking operations together, this will benefit the operation by having no waste between processes.

Question:
Linking processes together allows inventory to flow from one process to the next without _____. It is one of the seven wastes.

_____

_____

New Data Boxes & Design

- Operations brought together
- Scope of operator's job based on takt time
- Build new data boxes for future state map

- May be many traditional operations
- May have a unique design
- Focus on minimizing space and waste

Finish + Sub + Assembly

ENNA DATA BOX © Enna 2008
www.enna.com

Process: Finish + Sub + Assembly		# of Operators
Verb/Noun:		3

Operator Cycle Time: OCT	300 sec.
Machine Cycle Time: MCT	45 sec.
Value-Added Time: VAT	75 sec.
Changeover Time: C/O	N/A
Quality: % Defects/Scrap Rate	1%
Productivity: Units/Person/Hour	24/1/1
Total Space: Sq. Feet/Meters	80sqft
Value-Added Space: (sq.ft/m)	9sqft
Product Travel: Feet/Meters	35 feet
Product Flow: Push/Pull	Push Pull
Information Flow: Manual/Electronic	Manual Elec.
Shifts: NET Avail. Time (Sec.)	1 Net Avail: 25200
Inventory: INV	Before: 25 After: 5

Notes, Slide 50:

_____

_____

_____

_____

_____

_____

Tip:
Although the Data Box provided can represent many processes it may be necessary to draw out a new layout.

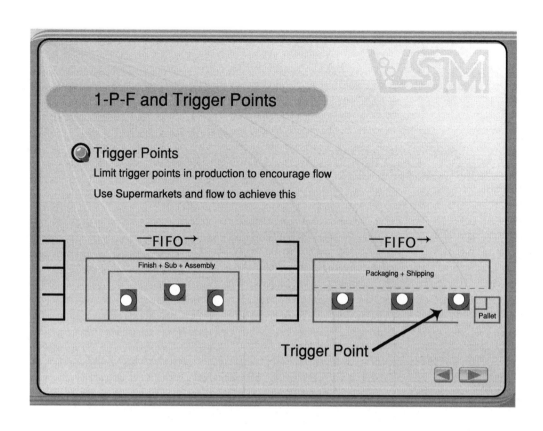

Notes, Slide 51:

_____

_____

_____

_____

_____

_____

Tip:
The goal, where possible, with redesigning and changing the way work is performed is to flow one piece of inventory at a time. When we have three processes linked together only one control point or trigger point is needed rather then three. The upstream processes just react to the downstream process.

Build to Supermarket / Shipment

- Use Supermarkets where you are not able to truly flow production.
- This is a "pull system" controlled by Kanbans.
- Start at the process closest to the customer and work backward through the logic.

Production Kanban   Withdrawal Kanban

FIFO→

Finish + Sub + Assembly

New Product   Withdrawn Product

FIFO→

Packaging + Shipping

Pallet

Notes, Slide 52:

Tip:
Supermarkets are only a last resort to workflow design. Use them only when absolutely necessary and should be viewed as temporary.

Build to Supermarket / Shipment

- Use Supermarkets where you are not able to truly flow production.
- This is a "pull system" controlled by Kanbans.
- Start at the process closest to the customer and work backward through the logic.

Production Kanban   Withdrawal Kanban

FIFO→   FIFO→

Finish + Sub + Assembly   Packaging + Shipping

New Product   Withdrawn Product

Pallet

Notes, Slide 52, Continued:

Tip:
Kanban systems allow the operation to control its own information without having to rely on a computer control system. As well, the information is truly customized for the operations that use the information.

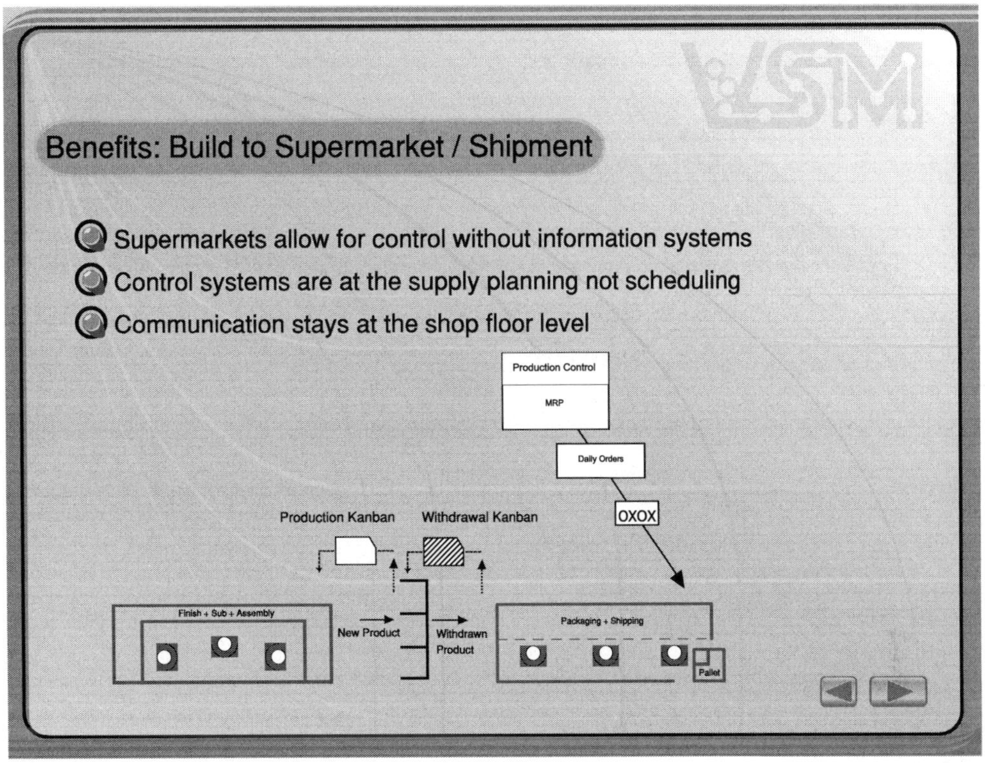

Benefits: Build to Supermarket / Shipment

- Supermarkets allow for control without information systems
- Control systems are at the supply planning not scheduling
- Communication stays at the shop floor level

Notes, Slide 53:

_____

_____

_____

_____

_____

_____

Question:

Kanban is simply a signal contained in a card format called a "signal card".

_____

Level Load Production Mix

- Foundation of Lean Manufacturing
- Averaging and standardizing are the foundational elements
- Level both the daily production volume and mix

Notes, Slide 54:

_____

_____

_____

_____

_____

Tip:
Level loading is balancing the operation based on production mix and production volume. It does not mean using batch production to smooth out the effects of demand.

Notes, Slide 54, Continued:

_____

_____

_____

_____

_____

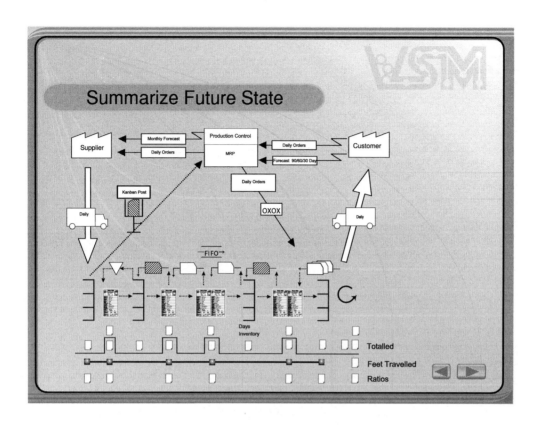

Notes, Slide 55:

_____

_____

_____

_____

_____

Suggestion:
Review the final map
before moving onto
the next slide.

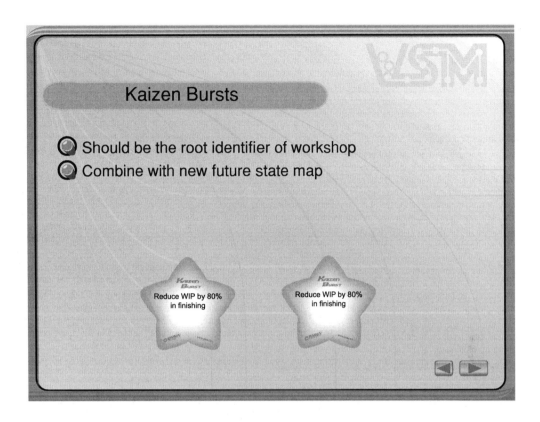

Notes, Slide 56:

_____

_____

_____

_____

_____

Tip:
Summarize the kaizen bursts for your future state map activities. Select the top ones to move forward with your implementation plan which follows in the next section.

Participant Workbook

Section 4

- Finalize Scope of Work for Workshops
- Establish Workshop Priorities and Sequencing
- Discuss Measurables for Each Workshop
- Establish Workshop Timeliness

 Suggestion   **Tip**   **Question**

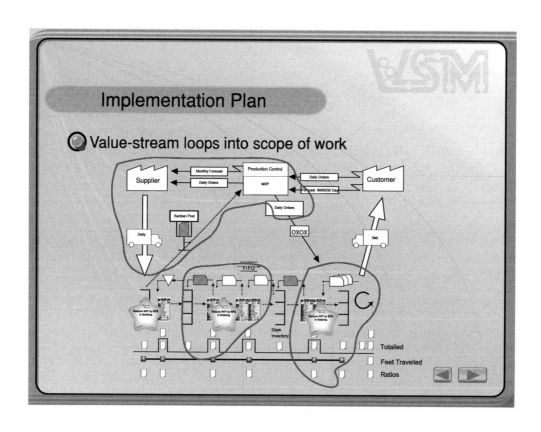

Notes, Slide 58:

_____

_____

_____

_____

_____

_____

Tip:
Discuss which area will be the pace setter for the implementation plan. Most often it is the processes just before shipping which will set the pace.

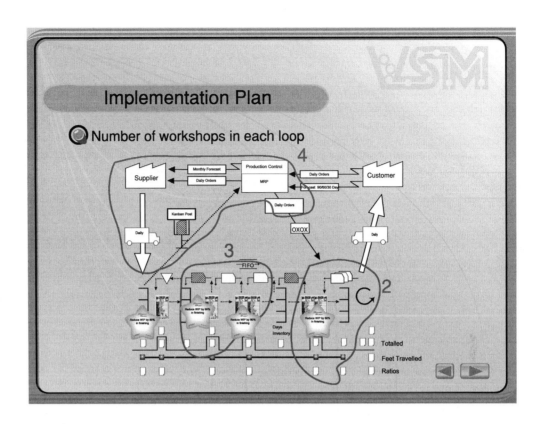

Notes, Slide 59:

_____

_____

_____

_____

_____

_____

Tip:
How many workshops will be needed to achieve the goals? This may also be the number of unique workshops in each general area.

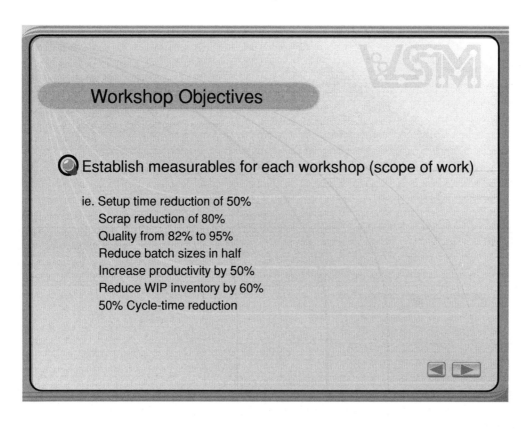

Workshop Objectives

○ Establish measurables for each workshop (scope of work)

ie. Setup time reduction of 50%
Scrap reduction of 80%
Quality from 82% to 95%
Reduce batch sizes in half
Increase productivity by 50%
Reduce WIP inventory by 60%
50% Cycle-time reduction

Notes, Slide 60:

Tip:
Focus on measurables which are generally accepted and have meaning to the team and the work area.

Question:
Ask the team which measurables will motivate change.

Establish a Workshop Plan

Establish an agreed upon timeline

Management, Maintenance, Engineering, Department, Human Resouces, etc.

Seasonality issues considering demand on production

Known production spikes

Known holidays and other constraints

Wainright & Johnson Inc. Gantt Chart - Winter 2008		Week 1 M T W R F 2 3 4 5 6	Week 2 M T W R F 9 10 11 12 13	Week 3 M T W R F 16 17 18 19 20	Week 4 M T W R F 23 24 25 26 27	Week 5 M T W R F 29 30 31 1 2
Workshop	Assembly					
	Prepare for Event					
	Notify Management					
	Notify Employees					
	Week Workshop					
	Followup Workshop					
Workshop	Finishing					
	Prepare for Event					
	Notify Management					
	Notify Employees					
	Week Workshop					
	Followup Workshop					

Notes, Slide 61:

Establish Membership

○ Identify departments necessary for workshop
Maintenance, Engineering, Department Sponsors,
Workshop leads, Outside contractors.

○ Review timing and frequency of workshops at the facility

○ Discuss workshop affect on organization
Human resources, capital requirements, delivery, etc.

Notes, Slide 62:

Current Value Stream Icons

The Inventory icon illustrates inventory between and before processes.

The Saw Tooth icon is used to help summarize key information such as cycle times, value-added times, and inventory days.

Operator icon shows the number of operators required in the area.

The Lightening Arrow icon represents electronic information flow: Internet, Intranets, LANs, WANs, EDIs, etc.

This is the Data Box icon. It represents a process, operation, or machine and is used to illustrate steps in the process.

The Solid Arrow icon represents physical flow of information; usually this is in the form of work orders to the shopfloor.

This is the Summary Note icon. It summarizes a number of critical measurements on the current and future state maps.

This icon represents planning or production control. This can be plant wide, department, area.

Supplier or Customer icon. Sarting point of material flow or ending point if it is the customer.

General Box icon is used for additional information.

This icon is used to illustrate control points and communication of information. This can be hourly, daily, weekly, etc.

These Black Outlined Arrow icons represent movement of material into the facility and out of the facility as finished goods to the customer.

Transportation icon to illustrate shipments from suppliers or to customers.

The Raw Inventory icon is used to illustrate the storage of large amounts of raw inventory before the process. Used to visually represent large amounts of storage before the value stream.

The Kaizen Burst icon is used to highlight improvement ideas as well as plan for future workshops.

The Dashed Arrow icon represents pushing material through from one process to the next process. Areas produce regardless of the needs of the next processes.

Future Value Stream Icons

This is an Inventory icon representing safety stock against factors such as spikes in customer demand or downtime on machines. This is intended to be a temporary solution.

This is an Inventory Stockpoint icon. When flow production is not possible upstream processes must be produced in batches. A stockpoint or supermarket is needed to allow for batch production and also to limit over-production and minimize WIP inventory.

The Kanban Post icon is used to temporarily store Kanban Signals for pickup. This is also used to exchange Withdrawal Kanbans and Production Kanbans.

The Withdrawal Kanban icon is used to provide instructions to the material handler to transport products or parts from the supermarket (stock point) to the downstream process. This Kanban instructs the material handler to withdraw a specific quantity and item.

The Production Kanban icon instructs the production of a specifically defined number of parts to be supplied to the downstream process.

Kanban Batch icon illustrates the movement of sequenced kanbans of a predetermined amount to the previous process. Once received, it triggers production of parts.

The Signal Kanban icon is used when the supermarket between two processes drops to a minimum trigger point determined by production lead-time. The Signal Kanban signals a changeover and production of a predetermined single batch of product.

OXOX

The Load Leveling (Level Loading) icon is used to re-sequence Kanbans in order to level production mix and volume over a period of time. This is often seen with the Batch Kanban icon.

The Pull icon represents a downstream pull to upstream processes. This indicates the physical movement of material downstream.

FIFO

The FIFO (First-In-First-Out) inventory icon is used as a process standard to use the oldest inventory first. This process is mostly used when multiple processes depend on each other and FIFO is required.

Value Stream Mapping Assessment

Facilitator:_____   Name:_____

Workshop:_____   Date:_____

Circle or write the answer that best fits the question or completes the statement.

1. **Value Stream Mapping is credited to __.**
   a) James Womack
   b) Mike Rother & James Womack
   c) John Shook & Mike Rother

2. **What company started what is now known as Value Stream Mapping?**
   a) Subaru
   b) Toyota
   c) Ford

3. **What are data boxes used for?**
   a) To collect data about MRP systems
   b) As a tool used by Toyota to calculate shipping times
   c) It is used in VSM to collect key process data

4. **Value Stream Mapping is concerned about isolating __.**
   a) movement, value-added, non value-added activities
   b) wastes, value-added, non value-added activities
   c) waste, excess processes, value-added activities

5. **Value Stream Mapping is a set of drawings that make the flow of __ and __ visible.**
   a) people and process
   b) material and information
   c) machines and inventory

6. **Value Stream Mapping is used to analyze the flow of material and information at __.**
   a) the enterprise, facility, and process level
   b) the facility, process, and machine level
   c) the country, regional, and state level

7. **Current State and Future State Maps illustrate the process as it is __.**
   a) today and illustrates the ideal state by applying Lean
   b) and illustrates the ideal state as it will be in six months
   c) today and illustrates the ideal state as it will be soon

8. **Value Stream Mapping changes your focus by __.**
   a) focusing on the value-added activities only
   b) showing how not to look at the operation
   c) focusing on waste reduction rather than value-added activities

9. **To map the Current State, there are __ steps.**
   a) nine
   b) eight
   c) six

10. **The Pareto Analysis form is used to__.**
    a) illustrate the quality and products in the operation
    b) illustrate the quantity and type of products in the operation
    c) illustrate recorded problems

11. **Briefly, the Histogram Analysis form is used to__.**
    a) research changes in customers' preferences
    b) consider varying changes in order batching
    c) consider cyclical changes in product demand

12. **During the use of the Product Family Matrix form you should group product families by __.**
    a) similar processes
    b) similar manufacturing functions
    c) similar department stages

13. **The Data Box is used to __.**
    a) record key information with regards to each process step that is being observed
    b) help observe processes selected during the discussions regarding value stream mapping
    c) help as a presentation tool only

14. **To develop a proper future state all design and workshop improvement should be based on __.**
    a) production batching constraints as determined by economic order quantity and yield rates
    b) machine cycle time and all operations balanced to this goal
    c) takt time and the balancing of operations to this goal

1:c, 2:b, 3:c, 4:b, 5:b, 6:a, 7:a, 8:c, 9:a, 10:b, 11:c, 12:a, 13:a, 14:c